The Palace of Westminster

KENNETH MACKENZIE, C.B.
SOMETIME CLERK OF PUBLIC BILLS
IN THE HOUSE OF COMMONS

NORWICH:
JARROLD COLOUR PUBLICATIONS

THE PALACE OF WESTMINSTER

The Old Palace

For more than nine centuries there has been a royal palace at Westminster, and the building which we call the Houses of Parliament is still a royal palace, partly controlled by the Lord Great Chamberlain, a Great Officer of State whose ancestors have held this office since Robert Malet in 1100.

That there was already a royal residence at Westminster in Saxon times seems probable, and there are some who say that it was here, on the banks of the Thames, not on the seashore, that Canute rebuked his courtiers for urging him to command the tide to go back. However that may be, the first palace of which we know anything for certain was built by Edward the Confessor between 1050 and 1065, at the same time that he was rebuilding Westminster Abbey.

The Confessor's palace stood between the river and the Abbey, and the space between the two buildings formed what later became known as Old Palace Yard. Nothing now remains of this palace, but the great hall (later known as the Painted Chamber) in which the Confessor is reputed to have died, survived into the nineteenth century. In 1834, when most of the ancient palace was burned down, the Painted Chamber, though damaged, was fitted up as a temporary House of Lords and the Lords continued to sit here until 1847, when it was pulled down to make room for the present Houses of Parliament.

Westminster Hall

Thus when William the Conqueror gained the throne, Westminster was already established as the centre of government. It was natural that he should be crowned in the Abbey, where the Confessor was buried under the high altar, and that when he held a great council in 1076 he should hold it in the palace built by the Confessor.

To his son and successor, William Rufus, however, the Confessor's palace did not seem grand enough, and in 1097 he ordered the building of a new palace on the edge of the marshy ground which is now called New Palace Yard. Rufus's new Hall was nearly three times as long ($239\frac{1}{2}$ feet) and more than two and a half times as wide ($67\frac{1}{2}$ feet) as the old Hall. But, if the legend is to be believed, even these vast dimensions did not satisfy his ambition. Seeing it for the first time on his return from Normandy, he declared it to be 'a mere bed-chamber' compared with what he had intended to build.

The Westminster Hall we see today is not as Rufus built it, but enough of his original walls has been uncovered to reveal that at a height of nearly twenty feet an arcade of small rounded arches, forming a continuous pattern with the windows, ran all round. What we do not know is how the roof was supported, since it is certain that such a width could not at that time have been covered in one span. It is generally supposed that there were two lines of pillars; perhaps the general effect was like that of one of the great French Romanesque basilicas.

The Hall which we now see was rebuilt by Richard II between 1394 and 1399. The old walls remained but the arcaded gallery disappeared. The Norman windows were replaced by perpendicular Gothic windows, and a string course, carved at intervals with Richard II's badge, a chained hart, ran below them. At the north end two towers were added and a porch with niches for statues and a great window above. But the most striking feature of the rebuilt Hall was the great roof. Henry Yevele, the first great exponent of the Perpendicular style, was the master mason who was responsible for the building as a whole. The hammer-beam roof was the design of Hugh Herland, son of the carpenter who designed the roof of the Great Hall at Windsor.

Richard did not have much joy of his great work. The building of the Hall had hardly begun when Queen Anne died at the age of twenty-seven. Distraught with grief, Richard halted all building operations, but orders were soon given to resume building with all speed. In 1396 Richard was married again, to Isabella, the seven-year-old daughter of Charles VI of France, and by 1397 the rebuilding of the Hall was sufficiently advanced to make it possible, with the aid of a temporary roof, to hold the coronation feast there. The riots at this feast, however, set Richard upon that violent course of action which led to his downfall. On 19 August 1399 he surrendered to Henry Bolingbroke at Flint Castle, and on 30 September before an assembly of Lords and Commons in Westminster Hall, Henry was acclaimed King.

From the earliest times Westminster Hall had been used for coronation feasts, and in fact it was so used at every coronation from Stephen to George IV. It may also have been used for meetings of those great councils from which Parliament developed, but the Hall has been more closely associated with the law courts. In the earliest times the courts had followed the King, wherever he was, but in the reign of Henry III, in 1224, it was ordained 'that there should be a standing place appointed, where matters should be heard and judged, which was in the Great Hall at Westminster.' Accordingly, by the late thirteenth century the Courts of King's Bench and Chancery were established in the south-east and south-west corners of the Hall respectively. The Court of Common Pleas sat near the middle of the west wall. The Exchequer Court found a home in a building outside the west wall. In 1825 the courts moved into buildings built by Sir John Soane on the roadward side of the Hall and remained there until 1882, when the Royal Courts of Justice were opened in the Strand.

In addition to its use by the ordinary law courts, Westminster Hall was the scene of most of the celebrated state trials and impeachments, including those of Sir William Wallace, Thomas More, Guy Fawkes, Charles I, the rebel Scottish lords of 1715 and 1745, and Warren Hastings. The last state trial held in the Hall was the im-

The House of Lords in 1755

peachment of Henry Dundas, Viscount Melville, in 1806.

Since the departure of the law courts in 1882, the Hall has had no specific function, but it has been the scene of many great national occasions. Gladstone, Edward VII, George V, George VI, Queen Mary and Sir Winston Churchill lay in state here; so also did the bodies of the forty-eight people who were killed in the airship R101 when it crashed near Beauvais in October 1930. The Hall has also made a noble setting for the presentation of Addresses by both Houses of Parliament, including those presented to George V at his Silver Jubilee in 1935, to the President of the French Republic and Madame Lebrun in 1938, to George VI in 1950 when the new Commons' Chamber was opened, and to President de Gaulle in 1960. In 1965 Addresses were presented to the Queen to celebrate the seventh centenary of the famous Parliament to which Simon de Montfort,

Earl of Leicester, caused to be summoned not only bishops, earls, barons and knights of the shire, but also, for the first time representatives of the cities and towns.

While Westminster Hall became the home of the law courts, the Confessor's palace became more closely associated with the meetings of Parliament. In the fourteenth century King, Lords and Commons assembled in the Painted Chamber for the opening ceremony, at which the Lord Chancellor, on behalf of the King, explained the reasons for summoning the Parliament. The Lords would then be ordered to assemble in the White Chamber on a later day to discuss the matters put before them. The Commons similarly would be told to withdraw to the Chapter House (or the Refectory) of Westminster Abbey for their discussions. Thus the White Chamber, a room at the south end of the Old Palace, became the House of Lords; but the Commons did not acquire a permanent room of their own within the Palace until after 1547.

St Stephen's Chapel

The Royal Chapel of St Stephen within the Palace of Westminster was suppressed by a statute of Edward VI in 1547 and soon afterwards handed over by him to the Commons for their permanent use. The original chapel, founded by King Stephen in 1141, had been pulled down in 1292 by Edward I, who began rebuilding it as a two-storied building in the manner of St Louis's Sainte Chapelle in Paris. The upper chapel, which was rebuilt after the fire of 1834 as St Stephen's Hall, was dedicated to St Stephen; the lower chapel, which survived the fire and is now usually called the Crypt Chapel, is dedicated to St Mary the Virgin. The building was finished in 1348 by Edward III, who founded the College of St Stephen, consisting of a dean and twelve canons. The interior was richly decorated with sculpture, wall paintings and stained glass, and there can be no doubt that in the words of John Carter, the antiquarian who saw what was left of it after the fire, the chapel 'must have been the first of all the architectural works of the land'.

Since it was a collegiate chapel it was not difficult to adapt it to the use of the Commons.

The Speaker's Chair was placed in front of the altar, rows of benches were substituted for the stalls and the ante-chapel became the lobby of the House. Thus the Commons, who had begun their collective life in the octagonal Chapter House, settled down in a room of the oblong shape which has come to be regarded as characteristic.

The Act of Union with Scotland increased the membership of the House of Commons from 513 to 558, and it became necessary to enlarge the Chamber, already too small for its membership. This was done under the supervision of Sir Christopher Wren, who installed galleries supported by pillars. At the same time he built a gallery for the public above the lobby, and covered the walls with oak panelling. In 1800 it became necessary still further to 'stretch' the Chamber to make room for the hundred Irish Members. The walls were cut away and the mural decorations were destroyed, but some idea

The House of Commons in 1741/42

St Stephen's Chapel after the fire of 1834

of their beauty may be gained from the reconstructions made by Professor Tristram.

For nearly three centuries, from 1547 to 1834, all the great events in English parliamentary history took place in this narrow chapel. It was here that the struggle for constitutional government was fought with the Stuarts by Eliot, Pym and Hampden; that Burke pleaded for an understanding of the American colonies; that Pitt and Fox contended on the questions of peace and war; that Wilberforce espoused the cause of the abolition of slavery; and that the long contest for the Reform Bill was carried through.

Barry's Houses of Parliament

On the night of 16 October 1834 a large part of the Palace was destroyed by a fire, caused by over-stoking the heating apparatus with Exchequer tallies. St Stephen's Chapel, the old House of Commons, was gutted, and the Court of Requests, where the Lords had been since 1801, was partially destroyed. Westminster Hall, the Crypt Chapel and Cloister Court were saved.

The Painted Chamber was fitted up for the House of Lords and the Court of Requests for the House of Commons; and in March a select committee of the House of Commons was appointed 'to consider and report upon such plan as may be most fitting and convenient for the permanent accommodation of the Houses of Parliament'. The Committee decided that the style should be Gothic or Elizabethan, partly because the new building had to be fitted into the surviving remains of the old one which was Gothic, and partly because it was believed that Gothic was essentially an English style. The design was put out to competition, ninety-seven designs were submitted and the winner was Charles Barry. His assistant was Augustus Welby Pugin, a man with a great gift for drawing and a passionate love of Gothic architecture. The question how much of the design of the Houses of Parliament is due to Barry and how much to Pugin has been the subject of much bitter controversy, but Sir Kenneth Clark's view seems conclusive: the plan of the building was Barry's, but 'every inch of the great building's surface, inside and out, was designed by one man: every panel, every wallpaper, every chair sprang from Pugin's brain, and his last days were spent in designing ink-pots and umbrella stands'. (*The Gothic Revival*)

The foundation stone of the new Palace was laid on 27 April 1840; the Lords occupied their Chamber on 15 April 1847; and the Commons first sat in theirs on 30 May 1850, but did not settle in permanently until the opening of the session on 3 February 1852. The installation of the clock and bells was not accomplished without a great deal of controversy. The clock did not begin its service until 31 May 1859, and the hour-bell, Big Ben, having developed a crack and been recast, was not hung and used until July of that year. After a few months further cracks appeared, but beyond giving the bell a quarter of a turn so that a different part should be struck and substituting a lighter hammer, nothing has been done and the cracks remain.

The Palace survived the First World War almost unscathed but was damaged on fourteen different occasions in the Second World War. Of these, the most serious was the air raid on the night of 10 May 1941, when, in the words of Winston Churchill, 'the enemy lit more than two thousand fires'. That night at least twelve incidents were recorded in various parts of the Palace and three people were killed. The Chamber of the House of Commons and the Division Lobbies were completely gutted by a fire which spread to the Members' Lobby. The roof of Westminster Hall was also set on fire but the prompt action of the London Fire Service prevented it spreading. The lantern and part of the roof boarding and rafters were destroyed, but the great trusses were not seriously damaged. The Clock Tower was struck and all the glass in the south clock face was broken, but the clock and bells were unharmed and the chimes were broadcast as usual.

The select committee appointed to consider the rebuilding of the Chamber chose Sir Giles Gilbert Scott, O.M., as the architect and once again late Gothic, though of a less elaborate kind, was preferred. The Committee were also insistent that 'the sense of intimacy and almost conversational form of debate encouraged by the dimensions of the old Chamber should be maintained'. Accordingly the floor of the new Chamber was made exactly of the same size as it was before, namely 68 feet long by $45\frac{1}{2}$ feet wide, but at the gallery level it was enlarged so as to provide 171 more seats for strangers and reporters. The number of seats for Members, of whom there are now 635, remained exactly the same as before, namely 437. The British House of Commons must be the only parliamentary assembly in the world which has deliberately provided nearly 200 seats fewer than there are Members. However, additional accommodation was provided for Ministers and Members in the form of secretarial, conference and interview rooms by utilising the spaces above and below the Chamber. The foundation stone was laid by Mr Speaker on 26 May 1948 and the Commons met in their new Chamber for the first time on 26 October 1950 in the presence of the Speakers or the Presiding Officers of twenty-eight Commonwealth legislatures.

Sir Charles Barry, 1795–1860, architect of the Houses of Parliament

The River Front

The Houses of Parliament *'are a triumph of the Picturesque. The long straggling line, the disproportionate tower, the monotonous detail – admit them all; but we cannot rid our imagination of that extraordinary building which seems to embody all that is most characteristic and most moving in London.'* (KENNETH CLARK, The Gothic Revival)

Parliament Square

Parliament Square is graced by a variety of historical figures, such as the statue of Sir Winston Churchill by Ivor Roberts-Jones which was unveiled by Lady Spencer-Churchill in the presence of the Queen in 1973.

The statue (*above right*) of Field Marshal Jan Smuts, Prime Minister of South Africa 1919–24 and 1939–48, is by Jacob Epstein and was completed in 1956.

The clock is commonly called Big Ben but the name properly belongs to the bell upon which the hours are struck. This great hour-bell, which weighs $13\frac{1}{2}$ tons, is said to have been named after Sir Benjamin Hall, a Welshman of vast girth, who was First Commissioner of Works in 1855–58. More probably it was named after Benjamin Caunt, the seventeen-stone prize-fighter, who in 1857, on his last appearance in the ring at the age of forty-two, fought sixty rounds, with the contest ending in a draw.

Old Palace Yard

Overlooking Old Palace Yard is the Chapter House of Westminster Abbey (*above*), used by the Commons in the fourteenth century. Across the Yard is the great south window of Westminster Hall and the House of Lords (*below*).

The State Opening of Parliament

On this State occasion the Queen and Prince Philip travel in the Irish State coach, escorted by Household Cavalry, on their ride from Buckingham Palace (*above right*) to the Houses of Parliament, and on the return journey (*below right*).

Richard Coeur de Lion

The statue of Richard Coeur de Lion (*above left*) is by Baron Carlo Marochetti, R.A. (1805–68). On 26 September 1940 the sword held aloft was bent by the blast of an enemy bomb – 'a symbol' said Mr Vincent Massey, the Canadian High Commissioner, in a broadcast to Canada 'of the strength of democracy which will bend but not break under attack'. The statue stands in Old Palace Yard close to the Peers' Entrance to the House of Lords (*above right*).

The Jewel Tower

The Jewel Tower (*opposite*), like Westminster Hall and the old clock tower in New Palace Yard, was the work of Henry Yevele, the 'deviser of the King's works of masonry', and of Hugh Herland who ordained the carpentry. It was built in 1365–66 to house Edward III's private treasure. From 1621 to 1864 it was used to store the records of Parliament, and from 1869 to 1938 it was occupied by the Standards Department of the Board of Trade.

The Victoria Tower

The Victoria Tower is 323 feet high to the base of the flagstaff. Here are stored the records of Parliament, some two million documents, including the original copies of all Acts of Parliament since 1497, endorsed in Norman French. These records may be consulted by members of the public through application to the Clerk of the Records.

When the Queen comes to open Parliament the State Coach drives under the great archway to the foot of the Royal Staircase. At the same time the Royal Standard is broken from the flagstaff.

After the ceremony it is replaced by the Union Jack.

The Union Jack is flown from the Tower from 10 a.m. to sunset on sitting days and on certain special occasions such as royal birthdays. On 20 April 1917 the Stars and Stripes was flown alongside the Union Jack to celebrate the entry of the United States of America into the First World War. Since 1966 the Tower has been floodlit at night.

Henry Moore's sculpture, entitled 'Knife Edge – Two-Piece', is just visible at the bottom of the picture opposite.

The Royal Staircase and the Queen's Robing Room

On the occasion of the State Opening of Parliament the Queen alights from the State Coach at the foot of the Royal Staircase (*left*), is received by the Great Officers of State and escorted up to the Robing Room (*above*), where she puts on the Royal Robes and the Imperial Crown.

In 1941, when the Commons' Chamber was destroyed in an air raid, the Lords gave up their own Chamber to the Commons and went into the Robing Room which was specially fitted up for them. The Lords stayed here until 1951, when they returned to their own Chamber after the completion of the rebuilding of the Commons' Chamber.

The Royal Gallery

While the Queen is robing, a procession is being formed by the Heralds and the Great Officers of State in the Royal Gallery, which leads from the Robing Room at one end to the Prince's Chamber and the House of Lords at the other. Here it is, a splendidly ornate room of remarkable proportions: 110 feet long, 45 feet wide and 45 feet high.

The side walls are adorned by two huge pictures painted by David Maclise in the 1860s. The one visible in the photograph is of the death of Nelson at the battle of Trafalgar. The other, not shown in the photograph, is of the meeting of Wellington and Blücher after the battle of Waterloo. The gallery also contains many portraits of members of the Royal Family since George III.

Apart from its use as a processional route for the Queen on her way to open Parliament, the Royal Gallery has been used for the trials of peers by the House of Lords. The last such trial was in 1935, and the Lords gave up their right to be tried by their peers in 1948. More recently the Royal Gallery has been used when the two Houses wished to give a joint welcome to the head of a foreign state.

The Prince's Chamber

This room takes its name from a room of the same name which adjoined the old House of Lords. The present Prince's Chamber serves as an ante-room to the House of Lords.

The dominating feature of the room is the massive marble statue of Queen Victoria by John Gibson. Around the walls twelve bronze bas-reliefs by William Theed represent the following historic events in the Tudor period: The visit of the Emperor Charles V to Henry VIII, Edward VI granting a charter to Christ's Hospital, Lady Jane Grey as a student, Sebastian Cabot visiting Henry VII, Catherine of Aragon pleading her cause, the Field of the Cloth of Gold, Sir Walter Raleigh spreading his cloak for Queen Elizabeth, Queen Elizabeth knighting Francis Drake, the death of Sir Philip Sidney, Mary Queen of Scots leaving France, the escape of Mary Queen of Scots from Loch Leven Castle, and the murder of Rizzio, Mary's Italian-born secretary.

Above the bas-reliefs the walls are lined by a series of portraits of historical figures from the Tudor period. These were executed by students of the Royal School of Art in South Kensington, London.

The Peers' Staircase

Opposite can be seen a fine example of Pugin's Gothic design.

The House of Lords

The picture on the previous two pages shows what the House of Lords looks like when it is arranged for an ordinary legislative sitting, with the Lord Chancellor's Woolsack in front of the Throne.

Below is the scene in the House of Lords just before the Queen reads the Gracious Speech from the Throne. On either side of the Throne one of the Great Officers of State bears the Cap of Maintenance and the Sword of State. In the foreground the judges sit on two red woolsacks.

Opposite, a close-up of the Throne shows the detail of Pugin's design in all its splendour.

PHOTO: *The Press Association Ltd*

The Woolsack

The Lord Chancellor, as Speaker of the House of Lords, sits on the Woolsack with the Mace behind him. The Woolsack is traditionally held to have been introduced in the reign of Edward III.

In the course of time the Woolsack came to be stuffed with hair, but in 1938 it was re-stuffed with a blend of English, Welsh, Scottish and Northern Irish Wool, and wool from the Commonwealth countries, given by the International Wool Secretariat.

In front of the Lord Chancellor's Woolsack can be seen the edge of the two woolsacks on which the Judges of the High Court sit at the Opening of Parliament.

The Peers' Lobby

At the beginning of a sitting the Lord Chancellor, preceded by the Serjeant-at-Arms bearing the Mace, goes in procession through the Peers' Lobby and enters the Chamber of the House of Lords by the doorway shown in the picture opposite.

The Central Lobby

The Central Lobby is the place to which a constituent who wishes to see his Member of Parliament is directed by the police. He writes his name on a green card at the desk which can be seen to the left of the arch in the picture opposite. This card is then taken to the Member by one of the door-keepers wearing evening dress with the silver-gilt badge of a royal messenger.

The Central Lobby is an octagonal room 60 feet across with a vaulted roof 75 feet high. The ribs are joined by some 250 elaborately carved bosses and the spaces between them are filled with brilliantly gilded and coloured Venetian mosaics. Four great archways lead to the various parts of the Palace. Above the arches are mosaic panels representing the patron saints of England, Scotland, Ireland and Wales. The Central Tower stands above the Central Lobby and rises to a height of 300 feet.

The arch shown in the picture opposite leads to the Lobby of the House of Commons and it is through this arch that Mr Speaker, preceded by the Serjeant at Arms bearing the Mace, passes on his way to the Chamber at the beginning of each sitting.

'Henry VIII and Catherine of Aragon before the Papal Legates at Blackfriars, 1529'
One of the historical pictures in the East Corridor, painted by Frank Salisbury in 1910.

The desire of Henry VIII to divorce Catherine of Aragon was the immediate occasion of his breach with the Papacy. The two cardinals appointed by Pope Clement VII to try the case as legates are represented in session, Wolsey (with the orange in his hand) and Campeggio.

Catherine pleads: 'I take God and all the world to witness that I have been to you a true, humble, and obedient wife, ever comfortable to your will and pleasure. . . . This twenty years or more I have been your true wife, and by me ye have had divers children, although it hath pleased God to call them from this world. And when ye had me at the first, I take God to be my judge, I was a true maid, without touch of man. And whether this be true or no, I put it to your conscience.'

'Lancaster and York'

This painting is by Henry Payne, 1910.

The picture represents the famous scene in the Temple Garden when Richard Plantagenet plucked a white rose for the Yorkists and John ·Beaufort Earl of Somerset plucked a red rose for the Lancastrians. The anecdote, for which there is no historical basis, derives from Shakespeare *1 Henry VI*, II. iv:

PLANTAGENET:

Let him that is a true-born gentleman,
And stands upon the honour of his birth,
If he suppose that I have pleaded truth,
From off this brier pluck a white rose with me.

SOMERSET:

Let him that is no coward nor no flatterer,
But dare maintain the party of the truth,
Pluck a red rose from off this thorn with me.

Statuary

Opposite can be seen Oliver Cromwell, Lord Protector 1653–58, by an unknown sculptor; James Keir Hardie, independent Labour Member 1892–95 and 1900–15, by Benno Schotz; and W. E. Gladstone, Prime Minister 1868–74, 1880–85, 1886 and 1892–94, by F. W. Pomeroy.

Committee Stairs

Further statuary lines the Committee Stairs (*above*), close-up studies of which can be seen overleaf. The chandeliers on the Stairs originally hung in the Court of Requests, which was temporarily used by the House of Commons after the 1834 fire.

'The Commons petition Queen Elizabeth I to marry'

In this painting (*opposite*) by Solomon J. Solomon, on the Committee Stairs landing, the Queen holds up a ring and says: 'With this ring I was wedded to the realm.'

Four Prime Ministers (*above and below*)

On either side of the Committee Stairs are statues of Lord Palmerston and Sir Robert Peel by Matthew Noble; William Pitt, a copy of Nolleken's bust by Sebastian Gahagan; and Spencer Perceval, after Nollekens.

The Old Table of the House of Commons

Below can be seen the Table which was used by the Commons when they were sitting in St Stephen's Chapel. It dates from about 1730. After 1800 it was moved to the oratory in the Cloisters, whence it was rescued during the fire of 1834.

The Table that Pugin designed for Barry's House of Commons was burnt in the air raid which destroyed the Chamber on 10 May 1941.

The Table is an essential part of the furniture of the House. At the end nearer the Speaker's Chair sit the Clerks who write the minutes from which the Journal is compiled. At the other end are the two despatch boxes between which the Mace lies, when the Speaker or a Deputy Speaker is in the Chair. Ministers speak from the despatch box on the Speaker's right, leaders of Her Majesty's Opposition from the box on his left.

The Clerkship of the House of Commons goes back at least to 1363, when Robert de Melton was appointed 'under-clerk of the Parliaments'. ('The Clerk of the Parliaments' is the head of the permanent staff of the House of Lords.) The traditional duty of the Clerk of the House is to make true entries, remembrances and journals of the things done and passed in the House of Commons. He is not responsible for recording the speeches of Members, though this distinction was not made clear until 1628, when the King, having expressed a desire to see a speech entered in the Journal, the House resolved that 'the entry of the Clerk of particular men's speeches was without warrant at all times'. The House did not sanction the reporting of debates until 1803, and in 1812 gave this job to a separate staff under T. C. Hansard, from whom the official report gets its name.

The Committee Corridor

The principal committee rooms are on the first floor, overlooking the river, and are approached through the Upper Waiting Hall (*opposite*). Here stands a statue of Disraeli by Count Gleichen.

The Grand Committee Room (*overleaf*)

The committee rooms are in daily use for the meetings of Standing Committees on Public Bills, Select Committees on Matters and Private Bill Committees. The larger committee rooms are also available for party meetings.

The Harcourt Room

The Harcourt Room is a dining room on the Terrace floor where Members and Officers of the House of Commons and Members of the House of Lords who were formerly Members of the House of Commons may entertain guests.

Before 1773 no food could be obtained in the building, but in that year John Bellamy was permitted to open a small room to supply provisions for consumption on the premises. Lord Rosebery, in one of the appendices of his *Life of William Pitt*, quotes a story told at first hand to Disraeli that Pitt's last words were: 'I think I could eat one of Bellamy's veal pies.' Since 1773 food has been obtainable at any time during the sittings of the House of Commons, and since 1848 the supplying of it has been in the hands of a select committee.

The pictures in this room include a view of Venice painted by Sir Winston Churchill about 1951; the rest are on loan from the Tate Gallery. The room takes its name from Mr Lewis Harcourt, who was First Commissioner of Works from 1905 until 1910.

The Lords' Library

The House of Lords possessed no library until 1826 when Sir John Soane fitted up one of the rooms in the old building. In the fire of 1834 the room was gutted but the books were saved by being passed along a line of soldiers to St Margaret's Church. The four beautiful rooms designed by Barry were occupied in 1848.

The library is mainly composed of legal and parliamentary works, but also contains representative collections of standard works of history and biography, English, French and Classical literature, and theology. In the Queen's Room are displayed documents from the House of Lords Record Office, such as the Petition of Right and the death warrant of Charles I.

The Strangers' Dining Room

Here in the Strangers' Dining Room, Members and Officers of the House of Commons may entertain their guests.

In the oriel window are displayed the mallet and chisels which were used by Henry Broadhurst, the stonemason who was a Member of Parliament 1880–1906 and Under-Secretary of State for the Home Department in 1886.

The Terrace

The famous Terrace where Members of both Houses entertain guests to tea and strawberries in the summer. Behind is the Speaker's House and Westminster Bridge. On 8 July 1946 King George VI, Queen Elizabeth and the Princesses Elizabeth and Margaret landed on the Terrace from the royal barge and watched the victory fireworks from the Lord Chancellor's rooms.

The Commons' Library

The Commons' Library, besides keeping up to date as a good working library, provides a research and statistical service for the use of Members. Here is one of the fine large rooms it occupies on the Terrace front.

'The Coronation of Edward the Confessor'

A reconstruction of one of the paintings with which Henry III adorned the Painted Chamber. The Chamber was built by Edward the Confessor, damaged by the fire of 1834, fitted up as a temporary House of Lords, and demolished in 1847.

'The Adoration of the Shepherds'

One of the wall paintings in St Stephen's Chapel, the magnificent building which Edward I began and Edward III completed in 1348. The wall paintings were covered with wainscotting by Sir Christopher Wren in 1707 and were rediscovered in 1800 when the walls were cut back to make room for the Irish Members. Copies were made, from which the above has been reconstructed.

Big Ben

The Clock Tower which houses Big Ben rises above the Speaker's Court (*right*). At the top of the tower is the Ayrton light (named after the First Commissioner of Works 1869–73), which indicates when either House is sitting at night. First floodlit in 1931 for the International Illumination Congress, the Tower has been floodlit every night since 1964.

The Speaker's House

The portrait at the top of the Grand Staircase (*above*) is of Henry Addington, Speaker 1789–1801 and Prime Minister 1801–04. He was the first Speaker to live in the Palace and began the magnificent collection of Speakers' portraits.

The Portrait of Winston Churchill

This portrait was painted by Sir Oswald Birley in 1946.

The fan vaulting is part of the corridor which forms a cloister round the well in the centre of the Speaker's House.

The Speaker's House (continued)

As soon as the Commons began to develop some sort of corporate activity, they must have chosen a spokesman or Speaker to report their answers to the King. In the Good Parliament of 1376, when the Commons met for the unusually long period of ten weeks, Sir Peter de la Mare emerged as more than a merely occasional mouthpiece, but the distinction of being the first Speaker of the House of Commons is traditionally assigned to Sir Thomas Hungerford who was chosen in 1377. Neither of these Speakers had the qualities of impartiality and independence which we expect from a modern Speaker – they behaved much more like the leader of a party. During the fifteenth century Speakers were usually men who had been in the royal service, and in the Tudor era, though formally elected by the Commons,

they were in fact royal nominees. It is to Arthur Onslow more than any other Speaker that we owe the establishment of the tradition of independence. For thirty-three years he maintained an attitude of unflinching impartiality and enforced the rules of procedure without respect for persons. When he retired in 1761 the House voted him a pension of £3,000. By an Act of 1791 the Speaker was given a salary of £6,000, and three years later George III gave one of the houses in the old Palace as a permanent residence.

The principal rooms in the Speaker's House are on the first floor and look out on the river or Bridge Street. In the Speaker's study (*below*), in the drawing room (*opposite*), and in the State Dining Room (*overleaf*) are portraits of Speakers from the seventeenth century through to the twentieth century.

Black Rod summons the Commons (*below*)
At the State Opening of Parliament it is the duty of the Gentleman Usher of the Black Rod to summon the Commons to hear the Queen's Speech. When he reaches the door of the House, it is slammed in his face by the Serjeant at Arms. He knocks three times, the door is opened, and he advances to the Table of the House, bowing thrice, and delivers his message commanding the attendance of 'this honourable House' in the House of Peers. Then the Speaker, preceded by the Serjeant at Arms bearing the Mace, leads the Members to the House of Lords.

The House of Commons (*overleaf*)
Barry's House of Commons was completely destroyed in the air raid on 10 May 1941. The new House was designed by Sir Giles Gilbert Scott.

PHOTO: *Fox Photos Ltd*

The Speaker's Chair

When the House of Commons was rebuilt after the war, the furniture for the new House was given by the countries which were then members of the Commonwealth. The Speaker's Chair (*left*), carved in black-bean wood, was given by Australia. The three Clerks' chairs in front of it were given by South Africa, and the Table of the House, of which the corner is just visible, was given by Canada.

A Division Lobby

The Division Lobbies are corridors alongside the Chamber. Members voting 'Aye' go out behind the Speaker's Chair, and pass through the Lobby on his right. Members voting 'No' go out at the other end of the Chamber into the Lobby on his left. At the far end of each Lobby there are two desks (*below left*), at which Clerks record the names of Members, while beyond the doors two 'Tellers' count Members as they leave the Lobby.

A Despatch Box

The two despatch boxes which lie on the Table of the House were given by New Zealand. They are made of pururi wood and bound in bronze (*above right*).

The Mace in the House of Commons

The Mace was originally an emblem of royal authority but has come to symbolise the power and privileges of the House. It is carried by the Serjeant at Arms before the Speaker when he enters or leaves the Chamber at the beginning or the end of a sitting, or when he goes up to the House of Lords. When the House is constituted with the Speaker (or a Deputy Speaker) in the Chair, the Mace lies on two rests on the Table; when the House goes into Committee on a bill, the Speaker leaves the Chair and the Serjeant at Arms places the Mace on two rests below the Table. The Mace at present in use was probably constructed from pieces of two maces made in 1660. It is silver gilt, measures 4 feet 10½ inches in length and weighs 16 lb. (*right*).

The Churchill Arch

The Churchill Arch (*far right*) joins the Commons' Lobby to the Chamber of the House of Commons.

It is so called because, when the rebuilding of the bombed Chamber was discussed after the war, it was Winston Churchill who suggested that this arch should be rebuilt with the damaged original stones, 'as a reminder', he said, 'to those who will come centuries after us, that they may look back from time to time upon their forebears who "kept the bridge in the brave days of old"'. The statue of Winston Churchill is by Oscar Nemon and the statue of David Lloyd George on the right is by Uli Nimptsch.

St Stephen's Cloisters

The Cloisters (*below*) were rebuilt between 1526 and 1529 by Dr John Chambers, Henry VIII's physician, Canon of Windsor and last Dean of St Stephen's before its suppression.

The upper storey shown here was almost entirely destroyed in the fire of 1834, but it was carefully restored along its ancient lines. The two stories are connected by a staircase which provides the usual entrance for the Members of the House of Commons.

Two of the Paintings in St Stephen's Hall

Right: 'Cardinal Wolsey and Sir Thomas More in the parliament of 1523 at Blackfriars by Vivian Forbes. Sir Thomas More, as Speaker of the House of Commons, rejects Cardinal Wolsey's demand for a grant without due debate by the House.

Below: 'King John and Magna Carta at Runnymede' by Charles Sims. King John gives unwilling consent to the Great Charter, which reaffirmed the rights of the barons and came eventually to be regarded as the foundation of the constitution.

St Stephen's Hall

St Stephen's Hall was built on the site of the Royal Chapel which, for the space of nearly 300 years, from after 1547 until it was destroyed in the fire of 1834, had served as the Chamber of the House of Commons.

Brass studs in the floor indicate the position of the Speaker's Chair and the Table of the House. The statues on either side are of great parliamentary debaters – Pitt is nearest on the right and Chatham just beyond.

Westminster Hall

Originally built by William Rufus between 1097 and 1099, the Hall that we now see was built by Richard II between 1394 and 1399.

The six statues of kings in niches on the wall are contemporary with the Hall, but the great arch and the south window beyond were designed by Barry when he built the new Houses of Parliament. The stained glass by Sir Ninian Comper commemorates the Members and servants of both Houses who fell in the last war.

The Crypt Chapel

The Chapel of St Mary Undercroft was begun in 1292. Neglected after 1547 but restored after the fire of 1834, it is now used for the marriages of Members of both Houses, the christenings of their children, and celebrations of Holy Communion.

Searching the Vaults

Since 1605, when Guy Fawkes tried to blow up Parliament, Yeomen of the Guard have searched the Palace vaults before every State Opening of Parliament.

85306 636 1

© 1977 Jarrold & Sons Ltd, Norwich.
Published and printed in Great Britain by Jarrold & Sons Ltd, Norwich. 177.
Photographs by Richard Tilbrook of Jarrolds.

PHOTO: *Fox Photo*